Gluten Free Cookbook for Busy People on a Budget
50 Delicious 30-Minutes-or-Less Recipes for Weight Loss, Energy & Optimum Health

by

Helen Marie

Dell Publishing House

Disclaimer

The recipes in this book are for information purposes only and are not meant as a diet to treat, prescribe or diagnose illness. Please seek the advice of a doctor or alternative health care professional if you have any health issues you would like addressed.

Table of Contents

Author Page

Since she was 12 years old, Helen Marie loved to cook. True to her roots, her Southern mother taught her the recipes from her past.

As she aged though, Helen read books from many countries regarding cooking healthier meals. Slowly she changed the way she cooked and made her recipes more health-conscious.

A mother of four who has always worked at home, Helen enjoys playing and rough-housing with her two girls and two boys.

Since the oldest boy loves to pin his brother down, threatening to drop spit on him, Helen will in turn, pin him down and give him a taste of his own medicine.

Loving the arts, Helen enclosed the garage and opened a shop for kids' crafts, making all the crafts herself. Her friends are always visiting and shopping in that store.

Of course, she keeps up with play time with her kids and her cooking. All her family appreciates the variety of foods she prepares, delicacies from almost every country in the world.

Introduction

My Personal Testimony

I've had a gluten intolerance for almost 20 years. Back then, I never found any recipes that tasted good. I had to drive forever to a grocery store that carried only a few gluten-free items. Those items were not only hard to find, they were extremely expensive.

At first I fought this dilemma and was determined I could lick the problem by eating only a little wheat. I ended up balled-over, crying in pain each time I cheated and ate something that contained gluten. Later I was diagnosed with celiac disease, which is quite crucial and demanded that I stay on a very strict diet.

The facts finally hit me. I understood that my condition was serious and knew I couldn't manipulate or fight it any longer. I had to eat only 100% gluten-free foods. Sometimes wheat stays in the body for up to several years so It might take a little longer in your case, like it did in mine. I hope you get this book, start making the recipes here and begin your journey to a lifestyle of weight loss, energy and optimum health.

Resigning that gluten-free foods were always going to be very expensive, I started making many of my own gluten-free food combinations. I tried one recipe after another. After many years of tweaking recipes I like, I decided to share some of my favorites with you. I invite you to join me on a gluten-free diet and see how much better and healthier you feel in six months.

What Is Gluten and Why Does It Cause Problems?

Gluten is a long and complex protein found in wheat and certain other grains such as:

* Barley
* Rye
* Spelt
* Semolina

It is what gives bread dough its 'elastic' consistency, and is widely used within the food industry because of its ability to thicken and add texture to food products.

Although gluten is not naturally found in milk, it is normal practice to add it to milk products to increase their shelf life. Care should be taken to ensure that any dairy products used are gluten-free.

The digestive systems of humans are not well-designed to digest gluten. While some people never notice any adverse symptoms when eating gluten in their diet, there are many people for whom it can cause significant problems. For these people the side effects can cause long-term health implications such as:

* Digestive issues like: IBS, bloating, gas, constipation and diarrhea.

* Headaches, migraines, brain-fog and an inability to concentrate well.

* Fatigue and fibromyalgia-related symptoms.

* Mood swings, depression, ADD and anxiety.

* Diseases such as: epilepsy, celiac disease, malnutrition, many autoimmune diseases, dementia, and even autism.

Ten Signs That Prove You Are Gluten Sensitive

More than 55 diseases have been linked to gluten, the protein found in wheat, rye, barley, spelt and semolina. Research estimates that 99% of the people who have either gluten sensitivity or celiac disease are NEVER diagnosed. It is also estimated that as many as 20% of the US population is gluten intolerant. If you think you might be one of them, check out the following symptoms:

1. Digestive issues such as bloating, gas, diarrhea and even constipation (Children are the most likely candidates to suffer from constipation after eating gluten.)

2. Fatigue, brain fog or feeling tired after eating a meal that contains gluten

3. Neurologic symptoms such as dizziness or feeling of being off balance.

4. Hormone imbalances such as PMS, PCOS or unexplained infertility

5. Migraine headaches or "foggy mind"

6. Keratosis Pilaris, also known as 'chicken skin' is mainly visible on the back of your arms. (This tends be as a result of a fatty acid deficiency and vitamin A deficiency

secondary to fat-malabsorption caused by gluten damaging the gut.)

7. Diagnosis of an autoimmune disease such as ulcerative colitis, Hashimoto's thyroiditis, rheumatoid arthritis, Lupus, Psoriasis, Scleroderma or Multiple sclerosis

8. Diagnosis of chronic fatigue or fibromyalgia (These diagnoses simply indicate that your conventional doctor cannot pinpoint the cause of your pain or fatigue.)

9. Inflammation, swelling or pain in your joints such as fingers, knees or hips

10. Mood issues such as anxiety, depression, mood swings and ADD

How to Test for Gluten Intolerance

The single best way to determine if you have an intolerance to gluten is to completely eliminate it from your diet for at least 2 -3 weeks, then reintroduce it.

Please note that gluten is a very large protein and it can take months, even years to clear from your system so the longer you can eliminate it from your diet before reintroducing it, the better.

The best advice is, if you feel significantly better after removing gluten from your diet and notice more energy, but feel worse when you reintroduce it, then gluten is very likely a problem for you.

To get accurate results from this testing method, you must eliminate 100% of gluten from your diet.

Can You Stay Off Gluten for Several Years, Then Reintroduce It Slowly?

Once a friend of mine who only had a gluten sensitive completely eliminated gluten from his diet for 5 years, then very slowly reintroduced it. The results: He lost energy, suffered from headaches, a "foggy mind", joint pain, numbness in his legs, arms and fingers. He stopped gluten totally before his symptoms got any worse.

These symptoms typically appear hours or even days after gluten has been ingested, a response typical for people who only suffer from gluten sensitivity, not with people who suffer from celiac disease.

Those with celiac disease suffer much worse symptoms, sometimes fatal.

How to Treat Gluten Sensitivity

Eliminating gluten 100% from your diet means just that: 100% elimination. Even small amounts of gluten from cross contamination or medications or supplements can be enough to cause an immune reaction in your body.

The 80/20 rule or statement saying, "We don't eat it in our house; just when we eat out", is a complete misconception. If you do that, you will have problems, either immediately or later.

An article published in 2001 stated that for those with celiac disease or gluten sensitivity who ate gluten only once a month increased the relative risk of death by 600%.

How to Avoid Gluten

Gluten is found in many of the products on our supermarket shelves. It comes under a guise of different names, which make it difficult to identify which products contain it.

Natural flavor, monosodium glutamate, emulsifiers, lecithins, and hydrolyzed vegetable protein, to name just a few, are some of the ingredients whose origins derive from gluten.

The only sure way to eliminate gluten from your diet is to cook from scratch, using fresh, natural wholefoods, and avoiding grains.

While this may seem like a tall order in today's busy world, where convenience is a top priority for many, it doesn't have to be that way.

In this book you will learn how to create quick, easy and delicious recipes that will be gentle on your body, your budget and your time.

Tips to Help Achieve Your Gluten-Free Diet

Making changes to an existing diet can be difficult at first, but with practice and a certain level of commitment, you will quickly find that it doesn't have to be as hard or complicated as you thought.

Organization is key with any changes and taking the time to plan your weekly meals will help you reap dividends in the end.

The following tips will help you keep to your budget and organize your time so you are not in the kitchen cooking for hours on end.

All the recipes in this book take 30 minutes or less to prepare and cook, and less time than that if you employ a few of the following basic strategies:

* Sit down once a week and plan out the meals for your week ahead. This will be a major benefit when you shop for food because you will know exactly what you need, which will help you maintain your weekly food budget.

* Make meals in bulk, doubling the recipes, then freeze the extra meals. If you do this every day for a week, you will have a weeks' worth of food in your freezer.

* Buy fruit and vegetables that are in season and local. Check your local farmer's market and you will often find that you will save money over your local supermarket.

* Buy in bulk where possible because this will often save you money.

* Check special deals in your weekly supermarket circulars because this too can often save you money. Be

sure to check them carefully though because sometimes they are not as good as they seem.

* Build up your pantry slowly, rather than go out and buy a huge amount of new ingredients all at once. New flours and baking ingredients have a long shelf life so you have the time to buy one a week, which is a lot kinder on your budget.

Recipes

Get-Healthy Breakfasts

Mini Crustless Quiches

Ingredients – makes 12 quiches

3 large eggs
½ cup shredded cheddar cheese
¼ cup diced red pepper
¼ cup diced onion
¼ cup frozen spinach
Pinch of salt

Directions

Defrost the spinach before you start, or pop the box in the microwave for 30 seconds at a time until defrosted, being careful not to burn. Place defrosted spinach on a kitchen towel and squeeze out the excess liquid.

Preheat your oven to 350 F/180 C.

Beat the eggs in a large bowl and add all the other ingredients. Mix together well.

Spray some mini muffin tins with non-stick cooking spray. Bake for 20 minutes.

If you don't have mini muffin tins, then use some mini fairy cake cases.

Nutritional facts – per muffin

Calories 34kcal
Carbs 0.5g
Fat 2.3g
Protein 2.4g
Sodium 61mg
Sugar 0.4g

Coconut Pancakes

Ingredients – makes 8 pancakes
½ cup almond meal – available in health food shops
1 cup coconut flour
2 tsp gluten free baking powder
1 tsp almond butter
3 ½ cups coconut milk
1 tsp chia seeds soaked in 1 tbsp water
½ cup coconut sugar
1 tbsp cinnamon
Coconut oil to cook

Garnish
Mixed berries

Directions

In a large bowl place the almond meal and sift the coconut flour and baking powder into it. Add the cinnamon and coconut and mix.

In a separate bowl whisk together the almond butter, coconut milk, chia seeds and coconut sugar.

Add the wet ingredients to the flour mixture and combine well. It will be a thick mix.

Warm a non-stick pan, and add the coconut oil.

Add a few spoonfuls of the batter to the pan and cook for 2 – 3 minutes until browned, then carefully flip.

Cook for another minute, then place in a bowl and keep warm in a low oven.

Continue until all the batter is used.

Garnish with the berries. Add a drizzle of maple syrup (as a rare treat if you feel so inclined) and serve.

Nutritional facts – per pancake

Calories 405kcal
Carbs 25g
Fat 3g
Sodium 46mg
Sugar 12g

Tip: – To save money, make you own almond meal and almond milk and use the milk as a dairy milk replacement.

Take ½ cup of almond and soak in water overnight.

Drain the water and add the almonds to a food blender with 1 cup fresh water.

Blend until smooth.

Strain the almond milk through a nut milk bag or a clean stocking.

Pour the milk into a glass jar and store in the fridge. It will keep for a few days. If using the milk for a sweet recipe, blend in some honey or other healthy sweetener such as Stevia.

Use the almond meal as called for in this recipe.

Note: Almond meal can be frozen so you can make the milk when needed, then freeze the remaining almond meal until you have a recipe that requires it.

Mexican Style Omelet

Ingredients – serves 4

1 tbsp olive oil
2 chorizo sausages – skin removed and cut into ½ inch slices
2 ½ cups cherry tomatoes, halved
2 tbsp jalapeno pepper, minced
1 tbsp garlic, minced
1.4 tsp salt
½ lime, juiced
4 tbsp unsalted butter
4 eggs
½ cup queso fresco cheese, or similar cheese

Garnish
Cilantro and chives

Directions

In a medium-size pan, add 1 tablespoon of olive oil. Cook the chorizo sausage for 2 minutes until browned.

Add the cherry tomatoes, jalapeno, garlic and salt. Cook for 5 – 10 minutes.

Beat the eggs and melt the butter in a frying pan.

Using a quarter of the egg mix at a time, pour into the frying pan and heat until the bottom side is set.

Carefully flip the omelet.

When cooked, add a quarter of the chorizo mix onto one half of the omelet, and add some cheese. Flip the other half over the top.

Continue until you have made all four omelets.

Top with the cilantro and chives, squeeze over the lime juice and sprinkle with any of remaining cheese.

Nutritional facts – per omelet

Calories 444kcal
Carbs 4.75g
Fat 39.5g
Protein 17.25g
Sodium 572.5mg
Sugar 3.5g

Gluten-Free Granola

Ingredients – makes 6 cups

2 cups walnuts
2 cups almonds
2 cups rolled oats
⅓ cup honey
⅓ cup grape seed oil or coconut oil
1 tbsp vanilla extract
1 tsp cinnamon
⅛ tsp nutmeg
¼ tsp salt (Use a good quality sea salt or Himalayan rock salt.)
1 cup dried unsweetened and shredded coconut

Directions

Overnight – soak your nuts in water because this makes them easier to digest.

Preheat oven to 300 F/150 C.

Drain nuts and pulse them in a food processor. Pour into a large bowl and add the oats. Mix together well and set to one side.

In a separate bowl, mix the coconut or grape seed oil, honey, vanilla, cinnamon and nutmeg.

Pour the wet mixture into the dry mixture and mix together well.

Line a baking sheet with parchment paper and spread your granola evenly over the tray.

Bake for 10 – 15 minutes. Remove from oven and stir over the granola. Place back in the oven for another 10 minutes, making sure to check on it often because it can burn quickly at this stage.

Remove from oven and allow to cool.

Stir in the coconut and place in a clean glass jar for storage.

Serve with fresh chopped fruit or berries and the almond milk from the previous recipe.

Nutritional facts – per 1 cup serving

Calories 636kcal
Carbs 46g
Fat 47g
Protein 17g
Sodium 4.5mg
Sugar 19g

Egg and Bacon Pockets

Ingredients – serves 4

For the Pastry

¾ cup millet flour
¾ cup rice flour
¼ cup arrowroot flour
¼ tbsp cornstarch
1 tbsp xanthan gum
1 cup butter
½ cup water

For the Filling

2 eggs
2 pieces of bacon
2 tbsp grated cheddar cheese

Directions

Mix the flours, xanthan gum and butter together in a food processor.

Pulse until the mixture looks like wet sand.

Place in a separate bowl and add the cold water a little at a time, making sure it is well mixed.

After you have added it all, cover and refrigerate for 1 hour.

While the pastry is cooling, scramble the eggs until barely set and place to one side.

Cook the bacon and crumble it into the eggs.

Mix in the cheese.

Roll out your pastry to ¼ inch thickness.

Cut into rectangles of 6 x 4 inches.

Place ¼ of the egg mixture into one half of each rectangle.

Fold the other half over it. Seal the edges with a fork.

Bake at 425 F/220 C for 15 minutes. Be careful not to over-bake.

Nutritional facts – per pocket

Calories 609kcal
Carbs 57.5g
Fat 35.5g
Protein 12.5g
Sodium 179.5mg
Sugar 0.5g

Mini Quinoa Muffins

Ingredients – makes 30 mini muffins

1 cup rolled oats
1 cup quinoa
1 cup walnuts
1 cup mixed dried fruits of your choice
⅓ cup brown sugar
1 tsp baking powder
3 tsp cinnamon
¼ tsp ground cloves
½ tsp salt
1 cup almond milk
2 tsp vanilla extract
2 tbsp coconut butter
2 eggs

Directions

Preheat the oven to 350 F/175 C.

Cook the quinoa in 2 cups of water. Set aside after all the water is absorbed and it has finished cooking.

In a medium bowl, mix together the oats, baking powder, spices and salt.

Stir in the walnuts and the dried fruit.

In a separate bowl mix together the brown sugar, milk, vanilla and softened coconut butter. Whisk in the eggs.

Add the dry ingredients to the wet ones and mix well.

Lightly grease your mini muffin tins, or use fairy cake cases if you don't have tins.

Spoon mixture into tins/cases.

Bake for 15 minutes until firm to the touch.

Nutritional facts – per mini muffin

Calories 90kcal
Carbs 12g
Fat 4.2g
Protein 2g
Sodium 20mg
Sugar 8g

Kedgeree

Kedgeree can be traced back to an Indian rice and beans or lentil dish called Khichri that dates to around 1340 A.D.

It is widely believed that British Colonials brought it back from India and presented it as a breakfast dish in Victorian times.

Ingredients – serves 2

4 oz cooked, long grain rice
2 oz cooked smoked haddock or cod
2 hard-boiled eggs
2 medium tomatoes
Olive oil
Seasoning to taste

Directions

Remove any skin and bones from the fish and flake into pieces.

Finely chop the tomatoes and 1 of the eggs, and add to the fish, along with the rice.

Heat the oil and add the kedgeree. Heat gently, stirring to avoid breaking up the fish.

Serve with the remaining egg, sliced on top for decoration, and with gluten-free toast if desired.

Nutritional facts – per serving

Calories 180.5kcal
Carbs 14g
Fat 6.5g
Protein 15.5g
Sodium 320.5mg
Sugar 3g

Oatmeal in a Jar

Ingredients – single serving

⅔ cup rolled oats
1 tbsp sliced almonds
1 tbsp dried cranberries or other dried fruit
1 tbsp chia seeds
1 tbsp ground flax (optional)
1 tbsp brown sugar
1 tsp cinnamon

Directions

Make up ahead of time by layering all the ingredients into a jar and sealing it with a tight lid.

If you are making it with the flax, jump to the next stage and add the milk. If not using flax, then this mix will last for several weeks in your pantry.

When ready to prepare, simply add 1 cup of milk (dairy or nut milk), and let sit in the refrigerator overnight (5 hours minimum).

In the morning, simply remove the lid and microwave for 60 seconds, or until desired temperature is reached.

Top with fruit, yogurt, honey or maple syrup.

Nutritional facts – per serving

Calories 380kcal
Carbs 60g
Fat 14g
Protein 14g
Sodium 56mg
Sugar 18g

Fruit Boats

Ingredients – serves 2

1 galia melon or other small melon
1 mango
½ pineapple
½ cup berries

Directions

Cut the melon in half and scoop out. Discard the seeds.

Scoop out the flesh and cut into small pieces. Place in a separate bowl.

Peel and chop the mango into pieces and add to the bowl of melon.

Peel and chop the pineapple into small pieces and add to the rest of the fruit.

Wash the berries and cut in half if necessary. Add to the rest of the fruit and mix together well.

Half the fruit mixture and place back into the melon skins.

Serve immediately or leave in the refrigerator to chill.

Nutritional facts – per serving (half of melon)

Calories 254kcal
Carbs 62.5g
Fat 0.5g
Protein 6g
Sodium 53g
Sugar 51.5g

Get-Healthy Lunches

Avocado, Tomato, and Cucumber Salad

Ingredients – **serves 6**

2 cups grape tomatoes (Use 2 cups cherry tomatoes if preferred.)
2 cups cucumbers, peeled and diced
4 cups avocados, diced medium
1 cup red onion, diced small
4 tbsp fresh cilantro, chopped
2 tbsp lime juice
2 tsp fresh garlic, minced
¼ cup olive oil
Salt and pepper to taste

Directions

Mix and serve by itself or over lettuce.

Nutritional facts – per serving

Calories 198kcal
Carbs 10g
Fat 18g
Protein 2g
Sodium 8mg
Sugar 4g

Avocado and Bacon Salad

Ingredients – serves 2

2 avocados
4 pieces bacon

Dressing

2 tbsp lemon juice
2 tbsp extra virgin olive oil
¼ cup apple cider vinegar
1 tbsp honey
Seasoning

Salad

Baby spinach and mixed salad leaves

Directions

Fry the bacon on a low heat until crisp. Set to one side.

Chop the avocado into small pieces. Set to one side.

Pour all the dressing ingredients into a blender and blend until smooth. Taste and season as needed.

Wash salad leaves and place in a serving bowl. Add bacon, avocado, chopped walnuts and mix. Pour over dressing and serve.

Nutritional facts – per serving

Calories 630kcal
Carbs 26g
Fat 57.5g
Protein 11g
Sodium 399mg
Sugar 9g

Summer Vegetable Pasta

Ingredients – serves 4

8 oz gluten-free pasta (try a brown rice fettuccini)
Salt and pepper
Olive oil
2 red peppers
2 ears of corn (or 1 cup golden corn from a can)
2 medium zucchini
1 cup cherry tomatoes, cut in half
1 cup basil leaves
4 oz goats cheese – omit if dairy intolerant

Directions

Boil a large pan of salted water and add the pasta, cooking according to the packet's instructions.

Chop the vegetables into bite-size pieces and cook in a separate pan over medium heat.

Heat the grill to a medium heat, and grill the corn until it starts to brown. Remove and set to one side. Or use the golden corn from a can.

After pasta is cooked, drain & save ½ cup of pasta water.

Add the vegetables to the pasta, with the tomatoes and the pasta water. Add the goat's cheese if using and the chopped basil leaves. Season well and serve hot or cold.

Nutritional facts – per serving

Calories 255kcal
Carbs 39.75g
Fat 7g
Protein 11.75g
Sodium 125.5mg
Sugar 6.25g

Spicy Cauliflower Soup

Ingredients – serves 6

1 head of cauliflower, broken into florets
1 red onion, cut into quarters
1 (15 oz) can garbanzo beans (or other white beans)
2 tbsp olive oil
Salt and pepper to season
⅓ cup gluten-free sunflower spread
½ cup water
1 tbsp gluten-free soy sauce
1 tbsp rice vinegar
1 tbsp brown sugar
1 garlic clove
1 inch piece of fresh ginger
½ cup cilantro leaves
Pinch chili powder (or more to taste)

Directions

Preheat the oven to 400 F/200 C.

Place the cauliflower, red onion and beans on a baking sheet and drizzle with the olive oil. Season to taste. Make sure you toss the ingredients into the oil well. Roast for 30 minutes, or until the cauliflower is tender.

While the vegetables are roasting, mix the sunflower spread with the water, soy sauce, vinegar, sugar, garlic, ginger and chili.

Add the sauce ingredients to a small saucepan and simmer the sauce gently until the sunflower spread has melted.

Place the roasted vegetables in a serving bowl and pour over the sauce. Toss well to coat all the vegetables.

Add the cilantro and serve.

Note: This soup can be eaten hot or cold and freezes well.

Nutritional facts – per serving

Calories 183kcal
Carbs 23g
Fat 8g
Protein 6g
Sodium 347mg
Sugar 5.5g

Arugula, Tuna and Cannellini Bean Salad

Ingredients – serves 8

¼ tsp Dijon mustard

3 tbsp fresh lemon juice

½ tsp minced garlic

¼ tsp kosher salt

¼ tsp freshly ground black pepper

1 ½ tbsp extra-virgin olive oil

1 cup grape tomatoes, halved

1 cup thinly vertically sliced red onion

1 (5 oz) package fresh baby arugula

2 (6 oz) cans tuna packed in olive oil, drained and broken into chunks

1 (15 oz) can cannellini beans, rinsed and drained

4 oz parmigiano-reggiano cheese, shaved

Directions

Whisk together the dijon mustard, lemon juice, garlic, salt, black pepper and olive oil in a large bowl. Add the tomatoes, red onion, arugula, tuna and cannellini beans. Toss. Top with cheese and serve.

Note: Terredora Di Paola Falanghina 2008 ($16) is a crisp and citrusy white wine with acidity to cut the flavorful oil in this salad. Light body and mineral nuance pair well with tuna, while a slightly peppery finish matches the herbaceous arugula.

Nutritional facts – per serving

Calories 175kcal
Carbs 12g

Fat 6g
Protein 19g
Sodium 342mg
Sugar 2g

Bean Soup

Ingredients – serves 6

1 (15 oz) can mixed beans
2 tbsp olive oil
1 large onion, chopped
2 large carrots, peeled and sliced
2 cloves garlic, crushed
1 lb spicy sausage, sliced
2 tbsp tomato paste
2 large potatoes, peeled and cubed
1 (14.5 oz) can diced tomatoes
½ head of cabbage, cored and thinly sliced
2 tsp balsamic or red wine vinegar
Seasoning

Directions

Heat the oil in a large saucepan or stockpot over medium heat.

Add the onions and carrots and cook for 5 minutes until they start to soften and brown.

Add the garlic and cook for 30 seconds.

Add the sausage and cook until browned, about 5 minutes.

Add the tomato paste, stir in well and cook for an additional 1 minute.

Add the beans along with 8 cups of water, the potatoes, cabbage, and the can of tomatoes. Stir together well.

Bring to the boil, reduce the heat and simmer for about 15 minutes or until the potatoes are tender.

Add the vinegar and seasoning and cook for an additional 1 minute.

Serve piping hot.

Nutrition facts – per serving

Calories 471kcal
Carbs 35g
Fat 26g
Protein 23g
Sodium 52mg
Sugar 9g

Vegan Crab Dip

This recipe is perfect for a light lunch or as a starter for a summer dinner party.

Ingredients – serves 6

1 (15 oz) can of white beans, rinsed and drained
½ cup vegan mayonnaise
¼ cup nutritional yeast
1 tsp dried or ground kelp
4 tsp bay seasoning – see below
1 lemon – juice and zest
2-3 dashes of tabasco sauce
1 bunch green scallions
1 (14 oz) can hearts of palm

Directions

Preheat oven to 350 F/180 C.

Add the beans, vegan mayonnaise, nutritional yeast, kelp, old bay seasoning, tabasco sauce, lemon juice and zest to a food processor and mix together well.

Add the scallions and pulse a few times.

Cut the hearts of palm into 1 inch pieces and add to the mixture. Pulse once or twice to break down a little, and create some texture.

Place the mixture into a ramekin dish or oven proof dish and bake for 30 minutes, or until it is heated through well.

Serve with vegetable crudities or make wraps from lettuce.

Nutritional facts – per serving

Calories 224kcal
Carbs 19g
Fat 12.5g
Protein 7g
Sodium 394mg
Sugar 0g

Note: If you can't find old bay seasoning where you live, you can make your own from the following recipe:

Homemade Old Bay Seasoning

1 tbsp celery seed
1 tbsp whole black peppercorn
6 bay leaves
½ tsp whole cardamom pod
4 whole cloves
1 tsp paprika
¼ tsp nutmeg

Directions

Place all the ingredients into a spice grinder or small food processor. Grind finely.

Use as called for in your recipe.

Creamy Asian Rice

Ingredients – serves 8

½ cup coconut milk
2 cups water
1 cup brown rice (uncooked)
4 tsp sunflower oil
2 tsp sesame oil
1 tsp hot chili oil, or ⅛ tsp crushed chili seeds
1 cup sweet red pepper
1 cup yellow onion
⅔ cup grated carrot
4 garlic cloves, minced
2 ½ tsp fresh ginger, minced
2 tsp cumin
Salt to taste

Directions

Add the coconut milk and water to a medium-size saucepan.

Add the rice and bring to the boil.

Reduce heat and simmer until all the liquid is absorbed.

Add the oils to another pan and sauté the onion, pepper and carrots for about 5 minutes (with a lid on the pan).

Add the garlic, ginger and cumin and mix well.

When the vegetables are tender, add the rice and mix well. Serve.

Nutritional facts – per serving

Calories 76kcal

Carb 9g
Fat 4g
Protein 1g
Sodium 10mg
Sugar 2.3g

Middle Eastern Pasta Salad

Ingredients – serves 5

½ lb gluten-free pasta
¼ cup tahini
⅓ cup water
¼ cup peanuts, shelled
Juice of ½ lemon
1 tbsp olive oil
1 clove garlic, minced
Salt and pepper for seasoning
1 cucumber
¼ cup red onion
¼ cup Kalamata olives, pitted and chopped
1 cup cherry tomatoes, halved
¼ cup mint leaves
4 oz feta cheese, crumbled (optional; leave out for dairy free or vegan)

Directions

Cook the pasta according to the packet instructions.

Rinse with cold water and drain. Set to one side.

Add the peanuts to a dry pan and cook over a medium heat for 3 – 4 minutes. Allow to cool and then chop coarsely.

Make the dressing by adding the tahini, water, lemon juice, olive oil and garlic into a blender and process until smooth. Season.

Peel the cucumber and slice in half lengthwise.

Scrape out the seeds and cut into ¼ inch slices.

Add the cucumber to a mixing bowl, add the onions, tomatoes, pasta and dressing.

Mix well and season if necessary.

Add the chopped mint leaves, peanuts and feta cheese. Serve immediately or refrigerate until needed.

Nutritional facts – per serving

Calories 523kcal
Carbs 74g
Fat 19g
Protein 12.4g
Sodium 289mg
Sugar 4.4g

Quinoa Mushroom Pilaf

Ingredients – serves 4

2 cups quinoa
1 tbsp olive oil
2 cloves garlic, minced
1 yellow bell pepper, diced fine
1 green bell pepper, diced fine
2 cups sliced mushrooms
Sea salt and ground pepper, to taste
2 tbsp fresh parsley, finely chopped
1 tsp Greek Seasoning (mint, lemon, basil, oregano mix)
2 scallions sliced
Squeeze of fresh lemon
Olive oil, to taste

Directions

Rinse the quinoa thoroughly and cook according to the packet instructions.

Heat the olive oil in a separate saucepan or skillet.

Add the garlic, yellow and green peppers, and stir over a medium heat until slightly softened.

Add the mushrooms and season with salt and pepper.

Add the Greek seasoning, and cook until the mushrooms are tender.

Add the cooked quinoa, and stir in the sliced scallions.

Mix well and squeeze fresh lemon and drizzle with the extra olive oil.

Nutritional facts – per serving

Calories 370kcal

Carbs 63.5g
Fat 8.5g
Protein 12.5g
Sodium 20.5mg
Sugar 1g

Get-Healthy Dinners

Parmesan Chicken

Ingredients – serves 6

6 chicken breasts
½ cup marinara sauce
¼ grated cheese
Olive oil

Directions

Preheat oven to 425 / 220C.

Place the chicken breasts on a baking sheet and drizzle with olive oil.

Bake for approximately 7 minutes until slightly browned.

Turn over and top with the marinara sauce and cheese.

Cook for another 5 – 6 minutes or until the chese has melted.

Serve with a green salad.

Nutritional facts – per serving

Calories 120kcal
Carbs 2.3g
Fat 2.1g
Protein 30.6g
Sodium 353.5mg
Sugar 1.8g

Shepherd's Pie

Ingredients – serves 4

4 medium potatoes
½ cup milk
½ cup grated cheese – cheddar is best
1 lb 90% ground beef
1 medium carrot
½ onion
3 tbsp butter
1 cup beef broth
1 tbsp corn flour (gluten-free)
2 tsp Worcestershire sauce (optional)
½ cup frozen peas

Directions

Peel the potatoes and cut them into small pieces. Place them in a saucepan of slightly salted water and bring to the boil. Simmer for about 12 minutes, or until cooked.

Peel and chop the carrot and the onion into small pieces. Heat a saucepan over medium heat and add a little oil to the pan.

Add the ground beef and brown for about 4 minutes.

Add the onions and carrots and cook for an additional 5 minutes. Add the peas in during the last minute or so of cooking.

In a small saucepan, make the gravy: Melt 2 tablespoons of the butter. Add the corn flour and mix together until smooth. Add the beef broth, and the Worcestershire sauce if using. Make sure the gravy is nice and smooth. Drain and mash the potatoes with 1 tbsp of butter, the milk, and some seasoning.

Pour the gravy over the beef and vegetables and mix together well.

Add the mix to an 8 x 8 inch ovenproof dish.

Top with the mashed potatoes and sprinkle with cheese.

Place under the broil for 5 minutes, or until the cheese is melted and golden in color.

Serve immediately.

Nutritional facts – per serving

Calories 407kcal
Carbs 32.25g
Fat 24g
Protein 17.5g
Sodium 229mg
Sugar 3g

Tomato and Parmesan Meatballs

Ingredients – serves 6

1 lb 90% ground beef
1 large egg
½ cup onion, finely chopped
⅓ cup grated Parmesan cheese
3 cloves garlic, minced
1 tsp dried oregano
1 tsp salt
½ tsp dried parsley

For the Sauce

¾ cup chopped onion
5 cloves garlic
¼ cup olive oil
1 (14 oz) can whole peeled tomatoes
2 tsp salt
1 tsp light brown sugar
1 bay leaf
2 tbsp tomato paste
¾ tsp dried basil
½ tsp ground black pepper

Directions

Preheat oven to 350 C/175 F.

Place all the ingredients into a large mixing bowl and using your hands, mix together well.

Roll into 1 inch balls. You should have enough mix for about 24 meatballs.

Place in an ovenproof dish and place to one side while you make the sauce.

Sauté the onions and garlic in the olive oil until soft and translucent.

Stir in the tomatoes, salt, sugar and bay leaf. Cover and simmer for 10 minutes.

Stir in the paste, basil and pepper. Stir well.

Pour the sauce over the meatballs and cook in the oven for around 15 – 20 minutes, or until the meatballs are no longer pink inside.

Note: These meatballs will freeze well.

Nutritional facts – per serving

Calories 281kcal
Carbs 5g
Fat 20g
Protein 19.5g
Sodium 91mg
Sugar 3g

Ginger and Garlic Stir Fry

Ingredients – serves 4

1 ½ lbs chicken breast, cut into small pieces
1 cup broccoli florets
1 carrot, peeled and chopped
½ red pepper, chopped
½ onion, chopped
1 zucchini, peeled and sliced
1 cup green beans
1 tbsp olive oil

For the Sauce

¼ cup gluten-free soy sauce
2 tbsp olive oil
1 tbsp dark brown sugar
1½ tbsp cornstarch
½ tbsp fresh ginger
2 cloves garlic

Directions

Whisk the sauce ingredients together and set to one side.

Heat 1 tablespoon of olive oil in a large saucepan or wok.

Cook the chicken until evenly browned. Set aside.

Add another tablespoon of oil and sauté the onions, pepper, zucchini, and green beans.

While they are cooking, microwave the carrots and broccoli for about 2 minutes. Or steam them for about 5 minutes until just tender.

Add the broccoli and carrots to the wok with the chicken and the sauce. Mix together well and allow the sauce to thicken.

Serve with brown rice.

Nutritional facts – per serving (without rice)

Calories 357kcal
Carbs 14.25g
Fat 12.5g
Protein 44g
Sodium 134.25mg
Sugar 5.5g

Gluten-Free Lasagna (Delicious!)

Ingredients – serves 8

1 box gluten-free lasagna noodles, uncooked
1 lb hamburger meat
1 large onion, diced
1 tbsp olive oil
1 (24 oz) jar spaghetti sauce
1 (12 oz) tub or bag Ricotta cheese
1 (12 oz) tub or bag Parmesan cheese
1 (12 oz) tub cottage cheese (optional)
Olive oil or other non-stick spray

Directions

Preheat oven to 350 F/175 C.

Heat skillet on medium. Add olive oil.

Scramble meat and onions in skillet.

Mix spaghetti sauce with meat and onion mixture and set aside.

In a 9 x 13 inch glass dish, spray bottom with olive oil non-stick spray.

Line bottom with uncooked pasta, probably 4 to 5 slices.

Spread out ½ meat/sauce mixture.

Sprinkle ½ of each of the cheeses.

Repeat the pasta, meat and cheeses. (Top should be the cheeses.)

Put in oven and cook for one hour. Some ovens vary, so you may need to cook for an hour and 15 minutes.

Remove from oven and let cool for 15 to 30 minutes so it sets.

Serve and enjoy.

Nutritional facts – per serving

Calories 678kcal
Carbs 56g
Fat 33g
Protein 42g
Sodium 1036mg
Sugar 8g

Sweet and Savory Pork Loin and Potatoes

Ingredients – serves 4

4 medium potatoes, peeled
4 boneless pork chops
3 tbsp olive oil
2 tbsp gluten free balsamic vinegar
Salt and pepper to season
8 cloves garlic
¼ yellow onion, sliced

For the Sauce

2 tbsp honey
¼ cup gluten-free chicken broth

Directions

Place the potatoes in a glass bowl and cover with plastic wrap.

Poke 4 holes in the plastic and microwave for about 10 minutes on a high setting.

Uncover and set to one side to cool slightly.

Heat oil in a large frying pan or skillet. Baste the pork chops with some balsamic vinegar and pepper.

Add the garlic to the pan and cook until aromatic. Remove and set aside.

Add the chops and brown each side for around 3 – 4 minutes. Set to one side, keeping them warm.

Cube the potatoes and add them to the skillet, stirring occasionally. Cook until slightly golden brown.

Add the onions and cook for about 2 minutes, until translucent. Set potatoes and onions to one side.

Using the same pan, make the sauce by whisking together the water, remaining balsamic vinegar, and the honey. Bring to the boil.

Add the chicken broth to thin if necessary.

Pour over the pork and potatoes and serve immediately.

Nutritional facts – per serving

Calories 535kcal
Carbs 44.75g
Fat 19.25g
Protein 44.5g
Sodium 392.25mg
Sugar 11g

Chicken Enchiladas

Ingredients – makes 12 enchiladas

1 package corn tortillas
3 chicken breasts
1 large onion, diced
2 (10 oz) cans red or green enchilada sauce
1 (8 oz) bag shredded cheese
1 large jalapeno, seeded and diced (optional; remember to wear plastic gloves)

Directions

Preheat oven to 350F/175C.

Cook chicken. Remove and shred.

Mix ½ can enchilada sauce with shredded chicken and onions.

Spoon a small portion on a corn tortilla, roll up and place in a 9 x 13 inch dish.

Repeat until you use all the chicken.

Pour remainder enchilada sauce over top of enchiladas.

Top with shredded cheese and jalapeno dices and cook for approximately 30 minutes, or until cheese is completely melted.

Serve and enjoy.

Note: You can also make this dish with hamburger meat.

Nutritional facts – 2 per serving

Calories 282cal

Carbs 24g
Fat 11g
Protein 24g
Sodium 703mg
Sugar 5g

Chicken, Potato and Cabbage Soup

Ingredients – serves 8 (so nutritious)

8 chicken thighs or 3 good-size chicken breasts
7 tbsp olive oil
14 medium-size Yukon Gold potatoes, unpeeled and cut into bite-size pieces
1 large onion, diced
½ to 1 bag mini baby carrots, cut in half
4 green scallions, chopped (optional)
1 (32 oz) box chicken or vegetable broth/stock
½ bunch Italian parsley (about 15 sprigs), medium chopped
¾ tsp ground cumin
½ tsp ground thyme
⅓ tsp crushed red pepper flakes (more if spicier soup is desired)
½ tsp poultry seasoning
4 cups water
½ medium-size head cabbage, washed and shredded
Sea salt and pepper to taste

Directions

Salt and pepper chicken pieces on both sides.

In a soup/stock pot heat 2 tbsp of olive oil on medium to medium-high heat, then add onions. Add salt to taste. Cook onions till translucent, approximately 6 – 7 minutes, stirring often. Remove onions, leaving olive oil.

Add remaining olive oil. Let heat for 1 minute.

Place the chicken thighs in that same soup/stock pot and cook them for 5 – 6 minutes on each side, or cook breasts for 6 – 7 minutes on each side. Remove and let cool.

While chicken is cooling add entire box of broth/stock to soup pot and turn on heat down to medium. Put onions back in.

Season with salt, pepper, cumin, thyme, red pepper flakes and poultry seasoning. Stir.

Add 4 cups water.

Add chopped scallions if using.

Add carrots and cook for 4 minutes, stirring frequently.

Add potatoes and continue to stir. Let cook for 4 minutes.

Add shredded cabbage and cook for 6 minutes.

While vegetables are cooking, debone chicken and cut into bite-size pieces.

Add chicken to pot and stir. Taste to see if soup needs more salt.

As soon as cabbage has cooked, remove pot from heat.

Ladle into soup bowls. Enjoy.

Serve with gluten-free crackers of your choice.

Nutritional facts (soup only)

Calories 317kcal
Carbs 66g
Fat 2g
Protein 19g
Sodium 373mg
Sugar 18g

Tuna Fishcakes

Ingredients – serves 2

2 (5 oz) cans of tuna (in water)
1 cup mashed potatoes (Use leftovers from a previous meal or make from scratch.)
1 egg
¼ cup gluten-free breadcrumbs
1 tbsp chopped herbs (basil and oregano work well)
Seasoning

For the Sauce

¼ cup light mayonnaise
1 tsp hot sauce
1 tbsp fresh lemon juice

Directions

Drain the water from the tuna and place in a bowl.

Break it up with a fork and mix in the mashed potatoes, beaten egg, herbs and 1 tablespoon of the breadcrumbs. Season to taste.

Divide mixture into 6 equal portions and make patties about 1 inch thick.

Place the remaining breadcrumbs on a plate and coat the patties evenly.

Place the patties in the refrigerator whilst you are making the sauce.

Add all the sauce ingredients to a bowl and whisk together well.

Preheat a large skillet or frying pan with enough oil to cover the bottom of the pan.

Fry each patty until golden brown, about 3 – 4 minutes on each side.

Serve with a green salad and a scoop of sauce on top of each patty.

Nutritional facts – per patty

Calories 622kcal
Carbs 78g
Fat 15.5g
Protein 47.5g
Sodium 840.5mg
Sugar 3.5g

Fast and Easy Chicken Quesadillas

Ingredients – serves 4

2 raw chicken breasts, cut into very tiny pieces
1 tbsp olive oil
1 (10 oz) can Rotel Chiles
½ (8 oz) bag shredded cheese (Mexican blend works best for this recipe)
8 corn tortillas

Directions

Heat a medium-size skillet on medium heat.

Add olive oil and raw, cut-up chicken. Cook until slightly white.

Add entire can of Rotel and cook until juice is gone. Place chicken in a bowl and set aside.

Clean skillet and heat on medium heat.

Place tortilla in skillet. Sprinkle layer of cheese.

Spoon chicken/Rotel mixture on top of cheese.

Add second layer of cheese.

Add second corn tortilla on top and cook until cheese has created a glue to hold tortilla in place. Flip and cook until bottom tortilla starts browning slightly. Remove from skillet.

Repeat 3 more times. Cut your 4 tortillas into 4 pieces each. Serve and enjoy.

Nutritional facts – per quesadilla

Calories 351kcal
Carbs 20g
Fat 15g
Protein 36g
Sodium 545mg
Sugar 4g

Vegetable Penang Curry

Ingredients – serves 6

2 tbsp olive oil
½ cup red onion, diced
1 tbsp fresh ginger, minced
4 garlic cloves, minced
4 oz mushrooms, washed, stemmed and sliced
⅓ cup sunflower butter
1 tbsp gluten-free curry paste
1 tsp ground turmeric
1 tsp ground cumin
2 tsp salt
1 tsp black pepper
2 tbsp brown sugar
1 (13.5 oz) can of coconut milk
2 cups water
1 small head of cauliflower
1 sweet potato
1 (15 oz) can chick peas
2 cups spinach leaves
1 lime, zest finely grated and juiced

Directions

Heat the olive oil in a large saucepan over medium heat.

Add the onions, ginger and garlic and cook for 2 – 3 minutes or until the onions start to soften.

Add the mushrooms and cook for an additional 4 minutes, or until they are browned.

Add the sunflower butter, curry paste, turmeric, cumin, salt, pepper, and sugar, stirring well.

Add the coconut milk, water, cauliflower, and sweet potato. Bring to a boil, and reduce the heat. Simmer for 20 minutes.

Stir in the chick peas, spinach, and lime zest and cook just long enough for the peas to heat through and the spinach to wilt.

Serve with rice or quinoa.

Nutritional facts – per serving (without rice or quinoa)

Calories 320kcal
Carbs 26g
Fat 21g
Protein 10g
Sodium 48mg
Sugar 8.5g

Fast and Easy Chicken Enchilada Soup

Ingredients – serves 6

3 chicken breasts, cooked and shredded
1 (32 oz) box chicken broth
1 (15 oz) can Ranch Style beans; can use 2 cans if
preferred (optional)
2 (10 oz) cans Rotel Original tomatoes (or different flavor
of your choice)
1 can red Enchilada Sauce
Tortilla chips

Directions

Mix all together and simmer for approximately 30 minutes.
Top with shredded cheese and crushed tortillas chips.
Serve and enjoy.

Note: Ground beef can also be substituted for chicken to
make Beef Enchilada Soup.

Nutritional facts – per serving

Calories 318kcal
Carbs 39g
Fat 11g
Protein 21g
Sodium 768mg
Sugar 3g

Grilled Tilapia with Garlic and Lime

Ingredients – serves 4

3 tbsp butter
2 – 3 cloves of garlic, minced
6 Tilapia fillets
1 tbsp old bay seasoning
¼ cup fresh lime juice

Directions

Melt the butter in a large saucepan over medium heat.

Add the garlic and cook for 1 minute.

Season the fish on both sides with the old bay seasoning.

Add to the pan and cook for 2 – 3 minutes. Flip and cook the other side for another 2 minutes.

Pour the lime juice into the pan and cover for 2 minutes, or until the fish flakes easily with a fork.

Serve with steamed vegetables and brown rice.

Nutritional facts – per serving (fish only)

Calories 229kcal
Carbs 1g
Fat 12.5g
Protein 30g
Sodium 114mg
Sugar 0.5g

Get-Healthy Desserts

Chocolate Orange Mousse

Ingredients – serves 2

2 ripe avocados
1 banana
2 - 3 tbsp unsweetened cocoa powder
1 tbsp of maple syrup depending on how sweet you want it
Juice of one orange
½ tsp orange zest

Directions

Blend the avocado, banana and cacao powder together until smooth. Taste and add some maple syrup if you want it sweeter.

Add juice of one orange and the zest and blend again.

Eat straight away, or chill in the refrigerator.

Nutritional facts – per serving

Calories 340kcal
Carbs 40.5g
Fat 22g
Protein 5.5g
Sodium 14mg
Sugar 16g

Lemon and Blackberry Mess

This is a rich and decadent dessert, not one for every day, but perfect for a quick, easy and delicious end to a dinner party.

Ingredients – serves 6

4 – 6 individual meringue cases
2 cups heavy cream
2 tbsp powdered sugar
10 oz lemon curd
2 cups blackberries (or any berries you like)

Directions

Whip the cream with the sugar.

Add the lemon curd to a bowl and whisk it to lighten it up.

Add ¼ of the cream to the curd and whisk. Fold in the remaining cream, mixing well.

Crumble the meringues so that you have some larger pieces and some smaller pieces for texture.

Using individual glasses, or one large serving dish, layer some of the lemon whipped cream into the bottom.

Next layer some of the meringue pieces, followed by the berries. Continue until you have used up all the ingredients.

This can be eaten immediately, or chilled in the refrigerator till later.

Nutritional facts – per serving

Calories 597kcal

Carbs 41.5g
Fat 41.8g
Protein 1.8g
Sodium 6.3mg
Sugar 48g

Blueberry Crisps

Ingredients – serves 6

Butter for preparing the pan
4 cups fresh blueberries
⅓ cup sugar
Zest of 1 lemon, finely grated
2 tsp fresh lemon juice
1 tbsp corn flour
⅓ cup dark brown sugar
⅓ cup gluten-free flour
¾ cup gluten-free oats
4 tbsp unsalted butter, softened
Salt

Directions

Preheat oven to 375 F/ 190 C.

Grease a 10 inch baking dish or a deep pie dish with butter.

Place the blueberries, sugar, lemon zest and corn flour in a mixing bowl and toss together well.

Pour mixture into the baking dish.

In a separate bowl, combine the sugar, gluten-free flour, oats and salt. Add the butter and work it in until the mixture is crumbly.

Spread over the blueberries and bake for 20 – 30 minutes, or until the blueberries are bubbling and the topping is golden brown.

Nutritional facts – per serving

Calories 405kcal

Carbs 49g
Fat 9g
Protein 2g
Sodium 8mg
Sugar 35g

Raspberry Fool

Ingredients – serves 4

12 oz raspberries
1 tbsp sugar
1 cup heavy cream
2 tbsp powdered sugar

Garnish

1 tbsp pistachios, coarsely chopped
4 sprigs mint

Directions

Place half the raspberries in a bowl with 1 tablespoon of sugar. Mash together with a fork.

Whip the cream with the powdered sugar until it forms stiff peaks.

With a slotted spoon, mix the mashed raspberries in with the cream. Do not mix in the raspberry juices.

Spoon half the cream/raspberry mix into 4 individual glasses.

Top with the remaining raspberries and cream.

Garnish with the pistachios and the mint.

Nutritional facts – per serving

Calories 287kcal
Carbs 19.25g
Fat 22g
Protein 2.75g

Sodium 0.25mg
Sugar 8.75g

Chocolate Brownies

Ingredients – makes 8 slices

6 tbsp gluten-free flour (for baking)
¼ cup corn flour
½ cup white sugar
½ cup soft brown sugar
6 tbsp unsweetened cocoa powder
½ tsp baking soda
1 egg
6 tbsp melted butter

For the Topping

½ cup sliced almonds
8 oz cream cheese (or dairy free alternative), at room temperature
⅛ cup sugar
2 tsp pure vanilla extract
Small can of cherries, chopped (you will want approximately 20 cherries)
½ oz dark chocolate, grated

Directions

Preheat the oven to 350 F/175 C and grease a 12 inch pizza pan.

Stir together the gluten-free flour, corn flour, brown and white sugar, and cocoa powder.

Whisk in the egg and melted butter so it forms a smooth batter.

Pour onto your pizza pan and bake for 10 – 15 minutes, or until a toothpick comes out clean from the center of the pizza.

Leave to cool.

Mix together the cream cheese, vanilla and sugar. Set to one side.

Toast the almonds, moving them around the pan constantly so they don't burn.

When the pizza base is cool, spread the cream cheese mix over it evenly and sprinkle to almonds and cherries over it.

Top with the grated chocolate and serve.

Nutritional facts – per slice

Calories 356kcal
Carbs 36g
Fat 21.8g
Protein 5.1g
Sodium 146mg
Sugar 28.75g

Luscious Lime Pie

Ingredients – serves 6

For the crust

2 cups nuts – walnuts or almonds work well
1½ cups shredded coconut
12 medjool dates (or more depending on the size of the dates)

For the filling

5 avocados
2 cups fresh lime juice
2 tbsp sweetener of your choice – or more to your taste
½ cup melted coconut butter

Directions

Make the crust by adding the nuts and dates to a food processor and process until you have a dough. Place mixture into an 8 inch pie dish and press until smooth.

Place in fridge to chill while you make the filling.

Add all the ingredients for the filling into your clean food processor and process until smooth.

Pour over your chilled base and return to fridge to set for 1-2 hours.

Nutritional facts – per serving

Calories 435kcal
Carbs 40g
Fat 32g
Protein 5g
Sodium 17.8mg
Sugar 25.5g

Hot Chocolate Cake

Ingredients – serves 2

3 tbsp butter
4 tbsp milk
½ tsp pure vanilla extract
1 large egg
4 tbsp sugar
4 tbsp unsweetened cocoa powder
4 tbsp gluten-free flour
¼ tsp baking powder
Whipped cream to serve (optional)

Directions

Melt the butter in a 12 oz microwavable dish or ramekin.

Swirl the butter around to ensure that all sides are coated.

Add the milk, vanilla and egg and whisk together well.

Add the sugar, cocoa powder, flour, baking powder and whisk together.

Microwave for 90 seconds or until the cake has risen and set.

Allow to cool slightly before serving with the cream if using.

Nutritional facts – per serving

Calories 373.5kcal
Carbs 21g
Fat 22g
Protein 7g
Sodium 100mg
Sugar 1.5g

Dairy-Free Ice Cream

Basic Ice Cream Mix

Ingredients – serves 4

8 frozen bananas

Directions

Chop bananas into small pieces and freeze.

Take frozen bananas and place in a food processor and process until they are creamy. You will know when they are done because their consistency changes from a frozen ice to cream – just like ice cream.

Serve.

Variations

Mint choc chip

Add a handful of chocolate chips or nibs to the bananas and a few drops of mint essential oil. Process as above.

Strawberry

Add 1 cup of frozen strawberries to the bananas and process as above.

Vanilla

Add 1 tsp vanilla extract to the bananas and process as above.

Chocolate

Add 1 tablespoon of cocoa powder to the bananas and process as above.

Nutritional facts – per serving of basic ice cream

Calories 210kcal
Carbs 54g
Fat 1g
Protein 3g
Sodium 2mg
Sugar 29g

Creamiest Rice Pudding

Ingredients – serves 4

1 ½ cups cooked rice, brown or white
4 cups dairy or almond milk
¼ cup blanched almonds (about 20)
¼ cup raisins
¼ cup currants
3 tbsp sugar
6 whole cardamom pods
2 inch piece cinnamon stick
1 tsp vanilla extract

Directions

Blend almonds with ½ cup of the milk until smooth.

Combine all ingredients in a large saucepan.

Bring to a boil, then reduce heat. Cover and simmer for 20 minutes, making sure there are no lumps.

Rice pudding will thicken more as it cools, so take care not to overcook it.

Remove cardamom pods and the cinnamon stick before serving.

Nutritional facts – per serving

Calories 269kcal
Carbs 48g
Fat 7g
Protein 5g
Sodium 48mg
Sugar 25g

Get-Healthy Snacks

Roasted Red Pepper Hummus

Ingredients – serves 4

1 (16 oz) can chickpeas
Juice of one lemon
2 tbsp tahini
4 cloves garlic, peeled
⅓ cup roasted red peppers, drain if using from a can
3 tbsp olive oil
2 tbsp fresh parsley or basil, roughly chopped
Salt to taste

Directions

Combine all ingredients in a food processor and process until smooth and creamy.

Taste and season as needed.

Serve with the gluten-free crackers.

Nutritional facts – per serving

Calories 245.5kcal
Carbs 24g
Fat 14g
Protein 8g
Sodium 293mg
Sugar 5.5g

Gingersnaps

Ingredients – makes 24 cookies

2 cups almond flour
½ tsp salt
½ tsp baking soda
1 tsp ground cinnamon
2 tsp ground ginger
¼ tsp ground nutmeg
4 tbsp melted butter
¼ cup honey
2 tbsp molasses
¼ cup candied ginger, finely chopped
1 tbsp light brown sugar

Directions

Preheat the oven to 350 F/175 C.

Line baking sheets with baking paper.

Whisk together the almond flour, baking soda, cinnamon, nutmeg and ginger.

Add the oil, honey, and molasses and mix well. Fold in the candied ginger.

Take a tablespoon of the dough and roll into a ball. Place on the baking sheet, spaced about 2 inches apart.

Flatten the cookies and sprinkle with the brown sugar. Bake for 12 – 15 minutes until the cookies are firm and the edges are just beginning to brown.

Nutritional facts – per cookie

Calories 92kcal

Carbs 7.8g
Fat 6.5g
Protein 2g
Sodium 1.8mg
Sugar 5.8g

Pistachio Chocolate Truffle Cake

Ingredients – makes 12 slices

1 tbsp butter
12 oz dark chocolate
8 oz heavy cream
3 tbsp gluten-free coffee flavored extract or liqueur
1 tsp vanilla extract
⅓ cup roasted, salted and shelled pistachios, coarsely chopped

Directions

Grease an 8 x 4 inch loaf tin with the butter. Line the pan with baking paper.

In a bowl, break the chocolate into pieces.

Bring the cream and extract or liqueur to the boil in a small saucepan, and pour over the chocolate. Stir in the vanilla extract and let it sit for 5 minutes for the chocolate to melt.

When the chocolate has melted, mix together well and pour the mixture into the loaf tin. Sprinkle the top with the chopped pistachio nuts and place in the freezer to set.

Nutritional facts – per slice

Calories 255kcal
Carbs 17.4g
Fat 20g
Protein 2g
Sodium 8mg
Sugar 13.5g

Coconut Macaroons

Ingredients – makes 8 macaroons

2 large egg whites
¼ cup honey
¼ tsp sea salt
2½ cups coconut flakes

Directions

Preheat your oven to 350 F / 175 C.

Whisk the egg whites with an electric mixer if you have one or a hand whisk if not until you have a stiff, glossy foam.

Carefully fold in the honey and the coconut flakes. Try to be as gentle as possible so the foam is not broken down.

Using a tablespoon or large serving spoon, take a spoonful of the batter and shape gently with your hand.

Place on a baking sheet covered with greaseproof/parchment paper.

Continue until you have used all the batter.

Place in oven and cook for 15 – 20 minutes until they are golden brown. The trick is not to overcook them because they will dry out. Your macaroons should be nice and chewy.

Nutritional facts – per macaroon

Calories 199kcal
Carbs 16g
Fat 15g
Protein 3g
Sodium 23mg
Sugar 12g

Mom's Delicious Homemade Salsa

Ingredients – makes 4½ cups

1 (6 oz) can tomato paste
1 large or 2 medium-size yellow onions, each cut into 8 pieces
5 or 6 medium-size tomatoes, as red as you can find but still firm
1 large jalapeno pepper
2 tbsp apple cider vinegar
1½ tsp minced garlic (best to use already minced garlic from store)
¼ tsp sugar
¼ to ½ tsp salt
3 tbsp water (optional; for thinner salsa)

Directions

Wash tomatoes and jalapeno pepper.

Put tomato paste in food processor.

Peel onion and chop into 8 pieces. Add to food processor.

Quarter tomatoes and add to food processor.

Slice jalapeno lengthwise, then remove seeds from each side. Chop into several pieces and add to mixture.

Add garlic, apple cider vinegar, sugar, salt and water to food processor. (Delete water if you like your salsa thick.

Blend till you have the size chunks you prefer, blending more if you like smaller pieces, less if you prefer it thicker and chunkier.

Take a spoon and stir around to see if there are any large pieces that didn't get mixed. If you find a lot of large pieces, blend a little longer.

Spoon into jars and refrigerate. Makes approximately 4½ cups. Serve with raw vegetables or chips.

Nutritional facts – per 3 oz serving

Calories 98kcal
Carbs 22g
Fat 0g
Protein 5g
Sodium 145mg
Sugar 13g

Tropical Trail Mix

Ingredients – serves 8

2 cups sliced almonds
1 cup unsweetened coconut flakes
1 cup macadamia nuts
1 cup roasted, salted pumpkin seeds
1 oz dried pineapples
1 oz dried mangos
1 oz dried strawberries

Directions

Place the almonds and coconut flakes in a large dry saucepan, over medium heat.

Heat, stirring often, until the coconuts and almonds are toasted and fragrant (about 6 minutes).

Allow to cool completely.

Place in a bowl and add the other ingredients. Mix together well.

Nutritional facts – per serving

Calories 490kcal
Carbs 21g
Fat 41.8g
Protein 14g
Sodium 11.8mg
Sugar 9.6g

Roasted Winter Nuts

Ingredients – serves 6

1 cup pecans
1 cup macadamia nuts
1 cup walnuts
2 tbsp flax seeds
1 tsp ground cinnamon
¼ tsp all-spice
1 tbsp sugar
¼ tsp salt
¼ tsp pepper
1 tbsp orange zest
1 tbsp olive oil

Directions

Preheat oven to 400 F/200 C.

Place all the nuts onto a baking sheet and dry roast for 10 minutes.

In a small bowl, combine the sugar and spices with the flax seeds and orange zest.

When the nuts are roasted, place them in a large bowl. Drizzle with the oil and spices and toss gently to combine.

Transfer to a warm serving dish and serve warm.

Nutritional facts – per serving

Calories 445kcal
Carbs 6g
Fat 46.5g
Protein 5.5g
Sodium 1mg
Sugar 1.6g

Grain-Free Crackers

Ingredients – makes 18 crackers

2 cups almond meal
1 tsp baking soda
1 tsp garlic, minced
Pinch dried onion
2 tsp dried Italian herbs
Pinch of turmeric or paprika for color
1 tsp sea salt
1 tsp sugar
1 cup finely grated parmesan cheese
2 tbsp olive oil
4 tbsp water (as needed)
1 beaten egg white

Directions

Preheat oven to 350 F/175 C and line a baking sheet with baking paper.

Combine all the ingredients in a mixing bowl and stir until you have a moist, moderately sticky dough. Add more water and oil if needed.

Taste and season accordingly.

Place the dough on your baking sheet and cover with another sheet of baking paper.

Using a rolling pin, roll the dough until it is about ⅛ inch thick. Remove top sheet of baking paper and if there are any cracks, simply press back into place.

Bake in the center of your oven for 15 minutes, or until the dough is cooked and golden.

Allow to cool and then cut into pieces using a pizza cutter.

Nutritional facts – per cracker

Calories 12kcal
Carbs 3g
Fat 9g
Protein 5g
Sodium 92.5mg
Sugar 0.7g

Crispy Kale Chips

Ingredients – serves 2

10 oz curly kale, stalk removed and torn into 2 inch pieces
(about 14 cups)
1 tbsp olive oil
¼ tsp salt

Directions

Preheat oven to 350 F/ 175 C.

Rinse and drain well. Pat off excess water with a paper
towel.

Place in a large bowl and pour over the olive oil and salt.

Massage the oil and the salt into the leaves until they start
to turn a more translucent color (this will become obvious
as you do it).

Spread the kale evenly over a baking sheet and cook for
15 minutes. Make sure you watch it carefully to avoid the
leaves burning.

Cool completely and store in an airtight container.

Nutritional facts – per serving

Calories 127kcal
Carbs 3g
Fat 8g
Protein 5g
Sodium 60mg
Sugar 0g

Conclusion

Shifting emphasis to a gluten-free diet can be a huge lifestyle change that many people look on with a sense of trepidation.

Thankfully, the reality is very different, and a gluten-free diet can be as full and delicious as meals you previously ate.

With a little planning and re-organizing of your pantry, it is possible to create time-saving, budget-loving, and most importantly, delicious-tasting recipes in your own kitchen. The truly great thing is that these are recipes your entire family will love, reducing the need to create something different for those in your family who can still eat gluten.

That said, even if someone doesn't show any outward signs of being intolerant to gluten, they will still benefit from taking a break and eating much less of it. Remember from our introduction how difficult a protein it is for the body to process.

I hope you enjoy creating the recipes in this book, and that it serves to make your transition to a gluten-free diet an easy and delicious one. Have fun.

Check out these other books by Sherry Everett under her pen names:

Upcoming books:

Lose Weight; Feel Great!: Eat These Delicious Meals to Get in Shape and Stay in Shape

Gluten Free Meals to Get in Shape: Eat Gluten Free for Optimum Health, Energy and Sustained Weight Loss

Busting 5 Healthy Food Myths: Foods You Must Avoid To Be Healthy: 30 Mouth-Watering, Healthy Recipes To Feed Your Family Well

and many more.

Review

Enjoyed this book?

Please leave a review below and let us know what you liked about this book by clicking on the Amazon image below.

and click on Digital Orders.

The above link directs to Amazon.com. Please change the .com to your own country extension.

Made in the USA
San Bernardino, CA
12 January 2018